A New True Book

CANADA

By Elma Schemenauer

CHILDRENS PRESS®
CHICAGO

Takakkaw Falls in Yoho National
Park, British Columbia

Project Editor: Fran Dyra
Design: Margrit Fiddle

PHOTO CREDITS

AP/Wide World Photos, Inc.—37 (right)

The Bettmann Archive—30, 34

© Cameramann International, Ltd.—13 (right), 14 (bottom
left), 25, 43 (left)

© Virginia R. Grimes—44 (left)

H. Armstrong Roberts—27 (top and bottom left)

Image Finders—© A. Flanagan, 15 (right)

© Bill Ivy—17 (right), 36, 38

Nawrocki Stock Photo—© Wm. S. Nawrocki, 25 (inset)

North Wind Picture Archives—28, 33

Odyssey/Frerck/Chicago—© Robert Frerck, 14 (bottom right),
15 (left), 19, 23 (right), 44 (right)

Photri—© Andrews-Orange, 43 (right)

© Porterfield/Chickering—Cover Inset, 27 (right)

© Carl Purcell—40 (left), 45 (center)

Reuters/Bettmann—37 (left and center)

Tom Stack & Associates—© Thomas Kitchin, Cover,
7 (2 photos), 40 (right); © Gary Milburn, 6, 17 (left);
© Victoria Hurst, 45 (left)

Tony Stone Images—9; © George Hunter, 13 (left), 18 (right),
21 (bottom); © Glen Allison, 14 (top); © John Edwards, 21
(top); © John Elk, 45 (right)

SuperStock International, Inc.—© Steve Vidler, 2; © Carl
Kummels, 12 (right); © George Hunter, 16 (right)

Valan—© Wayne Lankinen, 11; © John Eastcott/Yva
Momatiuk, 23 (left)

Reprinted with permission of Grolier [Canada] Ltd.—5

Maps by Tom Dunnington—10, 12 (right), 16 (right), 18 (left),
21 (right)

COVER: Moraine Lake, Banff National Park, Alberta

COVER INSET: Ottawa—capital city

Library of Congress Cataloging-in-Publication Data

Schemenauer, Elma.
    Canada / by Elma Schemenauer.
        p.   cm.—(A New true book)
    Includes index.
    ISBN 0-516-01065-4
    1. Canada—Juvenile literature.   I.   Title.
F1008.2.S34   1994
971—dc20   94-11943
                                                 CIP
                                                 AC

TABLE OF CONTENTS

THE NATION

Canada is the world's second largest country after the huge Russian Federation. It has an area of 3,851,809 square miles (9,976,175 square kilometers).

Canada stretches across the northern half of North America from the Atlantic Ocean to the Pacific. It extends from the Arctic

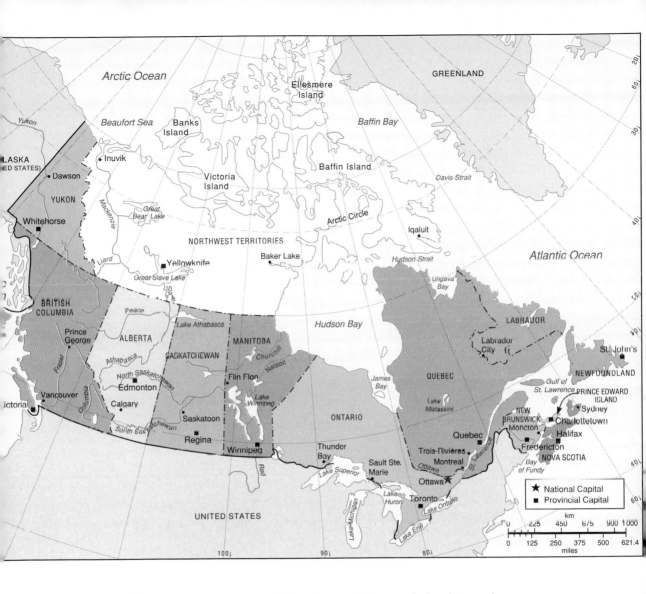

Ocean south to the United
States border.

Canada is a beautiful
land of many natural

5

Waterton Lakes National Park in Alberta

resources. It is known
for its huge forests, fertile
soil, and fishing grounds.
Many species of animals
live in Canada, and there
are deposits of valuable
minerals.

About 29 million people live in Canada. Only about five percent of the population work in rural areas. Many of them make their living by farming, ranching, fishing, trapping, mining, and forestry.

Cutting down a balsam fir tree (left) and processing salmon. Forestry and fishing are main industries in Canada.

Most Canadians work in cities and towns in the south. Some work in offices, stores, or banks. Others fix roads, build houses, or work in factories. And some are teachers, nurses, doctors, lawyers, or scientists.

Canada has ten provinces and two territories. In the east are the four Atlantic Provinces—Newfoundland, Nova Scotia, Prince Edward Island, and New Brunswick. In the west are

Ottawa, Ontario, is Canada's capital city. The government meets in the House of Parliament, the big green-roofed building in the background.

British Columbia, Alberta, Saskatchewan, and Manitoba. The largest provinces— Ontario and Quebec—lie between these two groups. The territories—Yukon and Northwest Territories— are north of the provinces.

Map labels: WESTERN MOUNTAINS · CANADIAN SHIELD · APPALACHIAN HIGHLANDS · GREAT PLAINS · GREAT LAKES— ST. LAWRENCE LOWLANDS

THE CANADIAN SHIELD

Canada has five main landforms. The largest is the Canadian Shield. This region lies around Hudson Bay like a huge ring. The Canadian Shield includes large parts of Quebec, Ontario, Manitoba, Saskatchewan, and the Northwest Territories. This

Lake Superior, the largest of the Great Lakes,
borders the province of Ontario.

area has many lakes and some forestland.

Most of the Canadian Shield is made of a hard rock called granite. It is generally too rocky for farming, but it contains valuable minerals, such as gold, silver, and iron ore.

The St. Lawrence Seaway at Montreal. Oceangoing ships sail the seaway from the Atlantic Ocean to the Great Lakes.

LOWLANDS AND PLAINS

Another main landform is the Great Lakes-St. Lawrence Lowlands in southern Quebec and Ontario. Farmers grow corn, wheat, tomatoes, apples, peanuts, and other crops there.

Lowlands occupations include farming and food processing. This farm is in Quebec, and this sugar plant (inset) is in Toronto.

The Lowlands are also Canada's main manufacturing region. People there make food products, toys, machines, computers, furniture, clothing, and other things.

13

Montreal, Quebec, is a beautiful city that combines modern skyscrapers with colorful old homes and sidewalk cafes.

Toronto, Ontario, is the largest
and fastest-growing city in
Canada. At left is City Hall
and its reflecting pool;
above, sailboats cruise on
Lake Ontario.

Canada's largest cities,
Toronto and Montreal, are
in the Great Lakes-St.
Lawrence Lowlands. These
cities are centers for
shopping, banking, trade,
and transportation.

Huge fields of wheat
stretch across the
southern parts of
Canada's Great Plains.

The Great Plains are
Canada's third main
landform. This region
includes much of
Manitoba, Saskatchewan,
and Alberta, as well as
part of the Northwest
Territories. The Great Plains
are vast grasslands with

few hills and trees. On the
rich soil of the south,
farmers grow wheat and
ranchers raise cattle.

Oil, natural gas, potash,
and other minerals are
found in the Great Plains.
Some Plains people work
in the mineral industries.

The city of Calgary (left) is in the province of Alberta.
Oil drilling and cattle raising (right) employ many people
in the Great Plains region.

A farm (right) on Prince
Edward Island

HIGHLANDS
AND MOUNTAINS

The Appalachian Highlands
include Canada's Atlantic
Provinces. The Highlands
are part of an ancient
mountain range. Worn down
by erosion, they are now
rounded hills.

18

The port of Halifax, Nova Scotia, is busy in winter, when the St. Lawrence Seaway is closed.

People in some parts of the Highlands work in mining, forestry, fishing, and farming. Many residents live close to the Atlantic Ocean. Scientists in the area also study marine life and the ocean floor.

The Western Mountains, Canada's fifth main landform, are high and rocky. This region covers most of British Columbia and Yukon as well as part of Alberta.

These mountains provide wood, coal, and copper. Milk, cheese, fruit, and other farm products come from the valleys. The Pacific coast provides fishing grounds.

Vancouver–in British Columbia–is Canada's third largest city.

Vancouver (above) is an important Pacific port. It is a center for trade with Japan and many other countries. A river (left) running through the Yukon Territory

THE MANY PEOPLES OF CANADA

Canada's first people probably came from Asia more than 20,000 years ago. They hunted, fished, and gathered plants and berries. These people were the ancestors of the Cree, the Ojibway, and many other First Nations in Canada.

The ancestors of Canada's Inuit probably came from Asia about 4,000 years ago. (*Inuit* means "people.")

Inuit grandmother and granddaughter (left). The totem poles above were carved by the Haida people of British Columbia.

They lived in the far north, where no trees grow. They fished and hunted polar bears, whales, seals, and caribou.

About 1,000 years ago,

Vikings came to Canada. They were the first Europeans who are known to have reached North America. They stayed for only a short time. Many years later, other Europeans arrived in Canada.

Today, many of Canada's people have European ancestors, including British, French, German, Italian, and Russian. The nation's population also includes people from China, India,

People from all over the world live in Canada, and many of them still speak their own languages. The stop sign (inset) is printed in Canada's two official languages English and French.

Africa, Australia, and South America.

Canada has two official languages–English and French. But many other languages are also spoken in Canada.

LONG AGO IN CANADA

In 1497, John Cabot explored the Atlantic coast of Canada and claimed the land for England. Cabot later told the English king that Canada's waters were rich in fish. The news brought many fishing boats from Europe.

A Frenchman, Jacques Cartier, was the first European to sail inland. In 1535, he sailed up the wide St. Lawrence River right into the heart of Canada.

Jacques Cartier (top left) and Samuel de Champlain (bottom left) explored Canada for France. Champlain founded Quebec City (above) in 1608.

NEW FRANCE

A few years later, France's Samuel de Champlain also sailed up the St. Lawrence. In 1608, he built a fort where Quebec City now stands.

27

He started the colony of New France.

French settlers and traders came to live in New France. Some farmed. Some traded pots, knives, and other European goods for the native people's furs. Most of all, the French

This view of a Hudson's Bay Company trading store shows native people and Europeans bargaining for furs and trading goods.

wanted beaver furs. These were sold in Europe for lots of money.

In those days, the French and English often fought each other. The English also had colonies in North America and wanted to keep them safe. They wanted to start new ones too. And the English Hudson's Bay Company wanted more beaver furs.

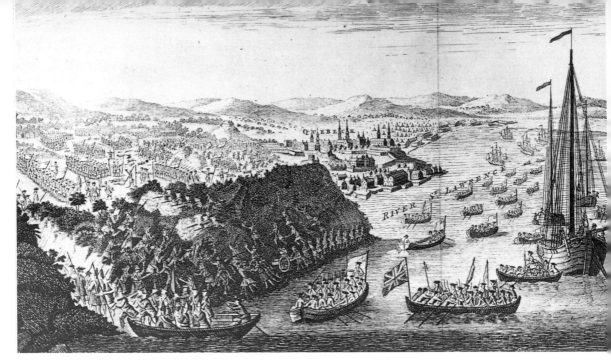
A painting of the Battle of Quebec, 1759. The British won the battle, and New France became British North America.

BRITISH NORTH AMERICA

In 1759, the French and the British fought their last great battle in North America. The British won, and gained the right to rule New France. Under British rule, the French kept their Roman Catholic religion and their French language.

Many new settlers then came to what is now Canada. They came from Britain, the United States, and many other countries. Many of the new people spoke English or other languages. Many belonged to Protestant churches.

OCEAN TO OCEAN

On July 1, 1867, the country of Canada was born. Four provinces of British North America joined to form the new country. They were Ontario, Quebec, New Brunswick, and Nova Scotia.

The British North America Act (the BNA Act) set up the new country's government. This act became Canada's

Opening the first Parliament of the new Dominion of Canada in 1867

constitution. It made Canada a democracy like Britain.

Each province had its own government, led by a premier. Canada also had a central government for the whole country. The

John A. Macdonald
played a leading
role in the
birth of the country
of Canada.

central government was
headed by a prime
minister.

John A. Macdonald
(1815-1891) became the
first prime minister. With
Macdonald as prime
minister, Canada grew.

Manitoba joined Canada as a province in 1870. British Columbia joined in 1871. Then Prince Edward Island joined in 1873. By 1885 trains were rumbling across the country, from coast to coast.

Canada kept growing. In 1905, Alberta and Saskatchewan joined. In 1949, Newfoundland became Canada's tenth province.

CHANGES

Pierre Trudeau

Canadians like to keep some ties with Britain. But by the 1980s, many Canadians, led by Prime Minister Pierre Trudeau, thought Canada should have its own constitution.

In 1982, the Constitution Act was passed. It ruled that Britain could no longer make or change any laws for Canada.

Some Canadians were not happy with the way the

When Prime Minister Mulroney (left) stepped down in the spring of 1993, Kim Campbell (center) became Canada's first woman prime minister. Jean Chrétien (right) became prime minister in November 1993.

Constitution Act was written. The government, led by Prime Minister Brian Mulroney, tried to change the act. However, most Canadians voted against the changes.

By the early 1990s, most Canadians were more concerned about jobs and trade with other countries.

Children arrive by bus for a day at school.

SCHOOL

Each Canadian province runs its own school system. Most have twelve grades. Canadian children start grade one by age six or seven. They attend classes from September to

June. They learn such things as math, science, language arts, social studies, music, and art.

Most Canadian schools are public schools. They are not linked to a religion. However, some religious groups have their own schools. Most of these are Roman Catholic schools. There are also Anglican, Christian Reformed, Jewish, and other religious schools.

Celebrations: Fireworks over Montreal (left) and a blueberry festival in Mistassini, Quebec

HOLIDAYS AND CULTURE

July 1 is Canada Day— Canada's birthday. On this holiday, Canadians have fun at parades and parties. They sing their national anthem, "O Canada."

Many Canadians work in the arts. Almost every Canadian city has stage plays put on by Canadian actors. Canadians also make films and recordings and paint pictures. Manitoba's Royal Winnipeg Ballet is one of the world's leading ballet companies.

Among Canadian writers known around the world are Farley Mowat, Jean Little, Mordecai Richler, and Margaret Atwood.

FOOD AND FUN

Canadians eat a variety of wholesome foods. Hot soup, beef, and fish are popular dishes for lunch and dinner. Many Canadians enjoy fast food. Hamburgers, pizza, and ice cream are favorites among young people.

Canadians also enjoy sports. Among their favorites are swimming, canoeing, biking, skating, curling, and skiing.

Professional sports in

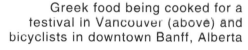
Greek food being cooked for a festival in Vancouver (above) and bicyclists in downtown Banff, Alberta

Canada include ice hockey, baseball, and football. Canadians follow their favorite teams on TV.

Canada has many national parks. There, visitors can enjoy sports amid the country's natural wonders. Alberta's Banff

View of Lake Louise in Banff National Park (left) and
"The Rocks" at low tide in the Bay of Fundy. The highest tides
in the world occur in the bay.

National Park is a favorite among skiers.

British Columbia's Pacific Rim National Park has miles of sandy beaches. Visitors come to watch sea lions and other Pacific Ocean wildlife.

And Fundy National Park

The people of Canada live together in peace, and work for a bright future.

in New Brunswick is the place to see the world's highest tides.

The people of Canada are as varied as their beautiful land. They are all working together to make their country a great place to live and work.

WORDS YOU SHOULD KNOW

ancestors (AN • sess • terz)–family members who lived earlier in history; grandparents, or forebears who lived long ago

beaver (BEE • ver)–an animal with long gnawing teeth and thick, dark brown fur

border (BORE • der)–an imaginary line that divides two countries, states, etc.

caribou (KAIR • ih • boo)–a deer with large antlers that lives in the northern parts of North America

colony (KAHL • uh • nee)–a settlement of people who have come from another country

constitution (kahn • stih • TOO • shun)–a set of rules or laws for the government of a group of people

curling (KERL • ing)–a sport in which heavy stones are slid down an icy track toward a round target

democracy (dih • MAH • kruh • see)–rule by the people or by representatives of the people

erosion (ih • ROE • zhun)–the wearing away of the land, caused by the action of wind and water

granite (GRAN • it)–a hard rock, usually gray or pinkish in color

landform (LAND • form)–the natural features or shapes of land surfaces

marine (muh • REEN)–living in the ocean

minerals (MIN • rilz)–substances such as iron, rocks, or gold that are found in the ground

potash (POT • ash)–a white substance that contains the mineral potassium; used in fertilizers and soap

premier (pree • MYEER)–the head of the government of a Canadian province

prime minister (PRYME MIN • is • ter)–the head of the government of a country that has an elected lawmaking body called a parliament

Protestant (PRAHT • es • tint)–a member of any of several Christian churches that are not allied with the Roman Catholic Church

province (PRAH • vince)–a division of a country, like a state of the United States

resources (REE • sor • sez)–supplies of valuable natural materials such as metals, gems, trees, water, or soil

Roman Catholic (RO • min KATH • lik)–a Christian church headed by the pope

territory (TAIR • ih • tor • ree)–an area of land that belongs to a certain country

Vikings (VYE • kingz)–people from northern Europe who were adventurers, sea rovers, and raiders

INDEX

About the Author

Elma Schemenauer is a Canadian author and former teacher who has written over fifty books. She enjoys travel, and has visited all three of Canada's oceans and most points in between.